How to Present an Evaluation Report

Lynn Lyons Morris
Carol Taylor Fitz-Gibbon

Center for the Study of Evaluation
University of California, Los Angeles

SAGE PUBLICATIONS Beverly Hills/London

The *Program Evaluation Kit* was developed at the Center for the Study of Evaluation, University of California, Los Angeles. Copyright of this edition is claimed until December 31, 1988. Thereafter all portions of this work covered by this copyright will be in the public domain.

The *Program Evaluation Kit* was developed under a contract with the National Institute of Education, Department of Health, Education and Welfare. However, the opinions expressed herein do not necessarily reflect the position or policy of that agency, and no official endorsement should be inferred.

The *Program Evaluation Kit* is published and distributed by Sage Publications, Inc., Beverly Hills, California under an exclusive agreement with The Regents of the University of California.

For information address:

Sage Publications, Inc.
275 South Beverly Drive
Beverly Hills, California 90212

Sage Publications Ltd
28 Banner Street
London EC1Y 8QE

Printed in the United States of America

International Standard Book Number 0-8039-1069-X
Library of Congress Catalog Card No. 78-58657

ELEVENTH PRINTING, 1983

Table of Contents

Acknowledgements

How To Present An Evaluation Report is part of the *Program Evaluation Kit,* developed over a three year period as a project of the Center for the Study of Evaluation (CSE), University of California, Los Angeles. The kit contains eight books, each covering a topic commonly confronting evaluators of educational programs. Many people besides the kit's authors contributed either conceptually or through technical support to its eventual publication.

We owe the idea of writing this kit to Marvin C. Alkin, Director of CSE from 1968 to 1975. Eva L. Baker, current Center Director, provided the continuing solid support and lively interest necessary for its completion. Adrianne Bank, first as co-director of the kit project in its early stages and then in her role as the Center's Associate Director, gave us the moral support necessary to traverse the arduous final stages of kit production.

Several staff members aided in the kit's extensive field test—151 sites throughout the United States and Canada. We thank Margeret Dotseth, Richards Smith Williams, and Esther Goldstein for their painstaking work in gathering and organizing field test data. The tone and content of the kit were strongly influenced by the comments of field test participants whose cooperation we gratefully acknowledge.

Significant editorial and conceptual work was done on this particular book by Marlene Henerson. Proofreading and indexing were handled by Michael Bastone, assisted by Mark Young.

Kit booklets were extensively reviewed by experts in the areas of evaluation research, methodology, and measurement. Comments about parts of this book were made by Ernest House, University of Illinois; Fred Niedermeyer, Southwest Regional Laboratory; Jason Millman, Cornell University; and James Burry, UCLA. These reviewers not only made valuable suggestions for revision of early drafts, but by either using the materials in classes with students or by discussing translation of technical issues into lay language, they gave the authors a strong sense of the kit's usefulness as both a procedural guide and educational tool.

We particularly thank Ann Moore Lee and Freda M. Holley for allowing us to include as Chapter 3 their compendium of tips for the evaluator, gathered over years of service to the Austin, Texas, Independent School District. The chapter is based on a paper delivered at the Annual Convention of the American Educational Research Association held in Toronto, March, 1978.

We wish to thank members of the Center's technical support staff who worked hard to keep manageable the production of such a large work. Donna Anderson Cuvelier carried the major responsibility for typing, organizing, and supervising manuscript preparation. Ruth Paysen ably shouldered part of the burden of typing the extensive manuscript.

Gracious thanks are also due Lou Orsan who provided advice about graphic design in the preparation of the field test draft of the kit and who designed the books finally published.

We wish finally to thank Cheryl Tyler of the UCLA Office of Contracts and Grants who ably ushered the kit through final legal channels toward publication.

Lynn Lyons Morris

Carol Taylor Fitz-Gibbon

Los Angeles, California
August 1978

Chapter 1

Introduction: Organizing Your Thoughts

The purpose of this book is to help you convey the evaluation information you have collected to your various audiences[1] as effectively and painlessly as possible. The book contains prescriptions and helpful hints for formal and informal reporting—either written or oral. The book's contents are based on the experience of evaluators at the Center for the Study of Evaluation, University of California, Los Angeles; on advice from experts in evaluation; and on the comments of people in school settings who used a field test edition.

In addition to this introductory chapter, *How To Present An Evaluation Report* has three sections. Chapter 2 presents a detailed but standard outline for an evaluation report. You can follow this outline to the letter, or you can simply use it to become familiar with the set of topics that should be discussed in an evaluation report. The outline is intended to be exhaustive of the type of information that can be conveyed to an evaluation audience. A glance at Chapter 2 will show you that each entry in the report outline is accompanied by a set of questions. These questions are intended to clarify each outline section and to help stimulate you to write. By answering the questions in sequence you will actually produce an outline of your evaluation report. Field test participants using this book found that the questions helped them to combat "writer's block."

Chapter 2, then, presents a fairly standard and, no doubt, familiar technical report outline. Depending on the stringency of your reporting

---

1. An evaluation *audience,* as the term is used here, is a group of people who have for one reason or another an interest in knowing your results. Most commonly, the audience will be the staff of the program's funding agency, and/or the people implementing the program itself. Sometimes you will need to explain your results to parents, community members, or others. Each of these audiences needs different information and different methods of presentation.

requirements, you may or may not decide to follow this rather formal method of presenting your evaluation and its results.

Chapter 3 should help you to organize your reporting methods for maximum impact. Consisting of a list of tips, Chapter 3 is a compendium of communication pointers. It includes advice on choosing what information to present to your various audiences. It gives pointers on good writing and effective verbal presentation, including a set of suggestions about what to do with a difficult or hostile audience. The purpose of Chapter 3 is to help you present the results of your work in ways which will most effectively convey the message of your evaluation.

A good strategy for using this book might be to begin by reading Chapter 2, using it to select and list the information you may need to deliver to interested people. Once this list is complete, decide which of the topics are likely to be of greatest concern, which will be most difficult to describe, which can be omitted, and which are likely to be misunderstood. Then read Chapter 3 and think about the various groups to whom you have to write or speak, looking for reporting methods that fit both what you need to say and your own strengths as a writer and reporter. Chapter 3 may provide you with ideas about grouping information in ways different from the outline in Chapter 2. You may decide, for example, that a report organized around salient questions in the minds of the audience would be the most effective method of conveying what your evaluation has discovered.

Chapter 4 helps you take advantage of the old picture-is-worth-a-thousand-words adage. It describes data presentation methods—tables, graphs, charts. Relying heavily on examples, it contains protypes of graphs and charts for displaying attitude, achievement, and program implementation data. To assist you with oral presentations, the chapter presents a step-by-step procedure for preparing audiences to read and interpret graphs.

You have great leeway in deciding what to report and how to say it. Evaluation is an evolving field, and there are few well-established procedures for collecting or for reporting evaluation information. There is serious doubt, for instance, about whether most audiences for evaluation reports can tolerate the deductively logical but usually dry presentations dictated by the classical report outline in Chapter 2. You might take this situation as a challenge to come up with effective presentation methods of your own. Your task as evaluator, after all, is to provide the best possible information to program funders, staff, and others with a stake in program processes and outcomes. Your obligation, therefore, is to gather the most highly credible information possible within the constraints of your situation and to present your conclusions in a form that makes them most useful to each of your evaluation's audiences.

Keep in mind, as well, that the prescriptions about reporting contained in this book represent what an evaluation report should contain *under the most advantageous circumstances.* Few evaluation situations, of course, match the ideal. Hopefully, you will examine the principles and examples provided and adapt them to the press of your own time and political constraints. Reading this book should at least help you to organize your thoughts about what you will say and how you will say it.

Evaluator Roles and Evaluation Reports

One critical factor determining the contents and format of your report is the nature of the role you as an evaluator have assumed with respect to the program. The *Program Evaluation Kit,* of which this book is one component, is intended for use primarily by people who have been assigned to the role of *program* evaluator. This means that your responsibility is to collect and report information about the effectiveness of a *program* as opposed to diagnostic data about particular students or information about the quality of the instruction given by individual teachers. Your role as program evaluator may vary in character depending on the task you have been assigned, but it will most likely resemble one of the two following descriptions:

1. You may have responsibility for producing a *summary statement* about the general effectiveness of the program. In this case, the audience for your report will be a funding agency, a government office, or some other representative of the program's constituency. You may be expected to describe the program, to produce a statement concerning achievement of the program's announced goals, to note unanticipated outcomes, and possibly to make comparisons with an alternative program. If these are the features of your job, you are a *summative evaluator.*

2. Your evaluation task may characterize you as a *helper* and *advisor* to the program planners and developers. During the early stages of the program's operation, you may be called on to describe and monitor program activities, periodically test for progress in achievement or attitude change, look out for potential problems, and identify areas where the program needs improvement. In this situation, you are a troubleshooter and problem solver whose overall task is not well-defined. You may or may not be required to produce a formal report at the end of your activities, but you will certainly need to talk with program people while you are working and at the conclusion of your work about what you have been able to discover. If this more loosely defined job role seems closer to yours, then you are a *formative evaluator.*

Summative Reports

If you are a *summative evaluator,* your report could affect important decisions about the program's future. This means that you must not only report the information you have collected, but you must also demonstrate to the audience that your measures and observations are accurate and that a true picture is being presented. The summative evaluator needs to defend the choice of evaluation *design,* as well as the *validity and reliability of the instruments* which have been purchased or constructed for the evaluation.

As a summative evaluator you will usually need to be careful of the credibility of your report and may have to present technical information. In most cases you should build your written report from the standard outline described in Chapter 2. If you have done such a thorough study that your report has the status of a *research paper,* then Chapter 2's standard outline should certainly be followed. If the report is to be submitted to a journal, the journal's own report outline probably matches the one in Chapter 2, though you should be careful to conform with the journal's stylistic idiosyncracies. Funding agencies often supply *their own outline* for the summative report. These outlines usually resemble the standard format.

Since the summative report is nearly always *written* and intended to be detailed, you should include as many charts and graphs as is appropriate to the task. A good table or graph with accompanying explanations, even when these explanations run to several pages, will help the audience understand some of the deeper technicalities sometimes explored in summative evaluation.

In spite of the fact that the summative evaluation report often carries the burden of communicating a lot of information, brevity and clarity are still important. For one thing, summative evaluations, if they are read at all, are usually scanned by administrative and legislative government staff advisors—who are extremely busy people. When asked what evaluators could do to make evaluation information more useful to State Assembly members, a legislative assistant once commented, "Just write down the conclusions of your report in one sentence, in large type, in the middle of a sheet of paper." Influential reports are short and to the point. While a single sentence cannot do full justice to your report, a short *executive summary* or *abstract* certainly can. This abstract should be written in straightforward language, perhaps organized around questions or graphic displays.

Formative Reports

If you are a *formative evaluator,* your reporting may affect important decisions about changes made in the program as it develops. The formative evaluator's fluid but constant relationship with the program makes it difficult to exactly prescribe the form of reporting required. For one thing, the formative evaluator reports to *program planners and personnel* who are familiar with the program, rather than to distant funding people whose only source of knowledge about the program is the report. In addition, formative reports usually occur frequently and may be informal and delivered orally. In many cases the formative evaluator is practically a program staff member, gathering opinions about preferred or more effective ways of installing the program; perhaps conducting short experiments to answer controversies that arise among the staff; and holding discussions to help the program planners achieve a comprehensive and rational statement of what the program is supposed to be doing.

In addition, the formative evaluator usually *monitors* the program, carefully examining it to describe the program that is evolving, to make periodic assessment of student achievement or attitudes, to assure that the program going on matches what was planned, or to gauge the adequacy of the plans in a real-world setting. These monitoring activities might very well require the formative evaluator to make periodic reports either orally before a group or in written form.

Conversations between formative evaluators and staff members, though they constitute reports, are not the sorts of things that a book on evaluation reporting can specify in advance. The major skills involved in giving and taking formative information have to do with *tact*—a personal quality resulting from experience in working with people—temperament, ability to listen, and genuine concern. Carl Rogers, communication experts, and others have written "How To" books on these topics. You are referred to these for help with informal conversation about the program.

If you find as formative evaluator that you need to present either a written report or a public presentation, there are some general strategies that can be followed. Formative reporting may take one or more of several forms:

Implementation reports. Most programs prescribe that certain crucial events occur. For example, students should be selected for participation according to certain criteria, particular books and materials should be used, specific curriculum units should be taught by certain people on or before a certain date, and so on. If such important events do not occur on schedule or if they occur in a way different, and possibly better, from what was planned, then corrective action may need to be taken, either in the form of modifying the activities occurring in the program or changing the program's written description.

One responsibility of the formative evaluator could be to map out and describe the materials and events in the program, either in writing or through discussions with the project personnel. The formative evaluator might therefore schedule periodic reports on program implementation. These reports must be *timely* and scheduled so that corrective action can be taken in time to remedy problems or so that changes in the program can be installed across sites. Whether an implementation report is formal or delivered in conversation, it should attend to the subject matter outlined for the *implementation* section of a formal report as described in Section IVB of Chapter 2[2]. If formative implementation reports are periodic, you might want to include answers to the following questions:

- What should have occurred since the last report?
- What has in fact occurred?
- What are the reasons for discrepancies, if any?
- What actions are recommended, if any?

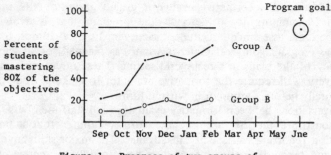

Figure 1. Progress of two groups of program students during a school year toward the overall goal of having 85% of the students master 80% (170) of the program's 212 objectives

Progress reports. Programs aim to achieve certain goals. It is not wise to wait until the end of the program before assessing goal achievement. The formative evaluator can regularly report student progress toward the program's general goals by watching for attainment of specific objectives or completion of selected program units. Reports about student progress should be *interpretive* as well as descriptive. That is, they should include projections, based on current progress, of the likelihood that a program will achieve its overall goals. Though projection of eventual results is not easy, graphs can sometimes help relate current results to eventual outcomes. For example, if a program goal is that 85% of the students will master 80% of the program objectives, a graph such as Figure 1—often called a trend graph—might be presented to a group of staff members at a meeting. Group B is clearly more in need of help than Group A, which

2. For a more detailed description of what to include in a formative report about program implementation, see Morris, L. L., & Fitz-Gibbon, C. T. *How to measure program implementation.* In L. L. Morris (Ed.), *Program evaluation kit.* Beverly Hills: Sage Publications, 1978.

seems likely to reach the goal. An accompanying list of *which* objectives or skills students have and have not mastered will encourage the staff to look for "bugs" in the program and to plan changes.

Measuring and interpreting progress will be easier if the formative evaluator has located or set up a control group. The experimental and control groups can be regularly monitored and contrasted. In the absence of a control group, the evaluator might examine data from previous years and use a rough longitudinal *time-series* design to help make cautious interpretations of current data. Information about graphing time-series data is also contained in Chapter 4, page 66.

In some cases, where program progress is considered critical enough to become a focus of constant public attention, the evaluator might consider using the *thermometer* common to fund raising campaigns. The thermometer in Figure 2 simply records the gradual progress of the program over time. But the thermometer, of course, fails to mention important information—such as which objectives have been mastered, how important they are, and so forth.

In general, the content of a progress report should cover such topics as those listed in Sections IVA and C of Chapter 2. Specifically, it should answer:

- What instruments were used to measure progress?
- Of what relevance and technical quality were these instruments?
- What progress has been made since the last report?
- Does this rate of progress predict success for the program?
- What features of the program appear to promote or hinder progress?
- What recommendations can be made for action, if any?

Technical reports. Problems that reflect a difference of opinion over the choice of procedures or materials for the program are particularly suitable

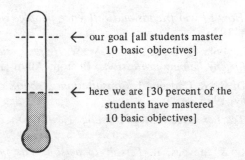

← our goal [all students master
10 basic objectives]

← here we are [30 percent of the
students have mastered
10 basic objectives]

Figure 2. A program progress thermometer

for handling by the formative evaluator. Would *Math Through Concepts* or *Let's Compute,* for instance, provide a more effective text for homework exercises? Will periodic student conferences maintain high attendance? A formative evaluator can conduct pilot studies and short experiments to answer such questions. Studies and experiments of this type usually include an experimental design and could be reported using the general outline of the technical report in Chapter 2.

Whether your evaluation role is formative, summative, or a little of both, your job as program historian is an extremely important one. People tend to believe what they see written down. Even staff members who work with the program every day will be influenced in their opinions by what you say. Whoever writes the report describing the program has great potential influence. What he says might well determine whether the program will continue as is, be changed, or perhaps be dropped.

For Further Reading

...On conventions and formats for writing reports:

Campbell, M. G., & Ballow, S. V. *Form and style: Theses, reports, term papers.* Boston: Houghton Mifflin Co., 1974.

Publication manual of the American Psychological Association. Washington, D.C.: American Psychological Association, 1974.

University of Chicago. *A manual of style* (Revised and enlarged). Chicago: University of Chicago Press, 1969.

U.S. Government Printing Office. *Style manual* (Rev. ed.). Washington, D.C.: Author, 1973.

...About communication in general:

Brown, G. *Human teaching for human learning.* New York: Viking Press, 1971.

Carnegie, D. *How to win friends and influence people.* New York: Simon & Schuster, 1936.

Combs, A. W., Avila, D. L., & Purkey, W. W. *Helping relationships: Basic concepts for the helping professions.* Boston: Allyn and Bacon, 1971.

Dinkmeyer, D. C., & Carlson, J. *Consultation: A book of readings.* New York: Wiley, 1975.

Gordon, L. *Teacher effectiveness training.* New York: Peter H. Wyden, 1974.

Rogers, C. R., & Stevens, B. *Person to person: The problem of being human.* Lafayette, CA: Real People Press, 1970.

Chapter 2

An Evaluation Report Outline

This chapter presents an outline of an evaluation report. As was mentioned in Chapter 1, the outline is meant to be used in one of several ways. If you are required to write a technical report—a likely event in summative evaluation or research—then your report will follow the outline here. Simply name each section of your report according to the headings listed, and answer the questions under each heading in as much detail as you feel necessary. This exercise will give you a working draft of the report.

On the other hand, if the form of your report is not prescribed, or if your reporting can be less formal, then you will use this chapter differently—as a *checklist* of contents for an evaluation report. You can then organize what you say according to your own needs, with the assurance that you are not omitting important information.

Whatever the case, consider the outline as suggestive, and drop questions, perhaps amplify some of them, or add your own questions as you see fit.

Front Cover

The front cover should provide the following identifying information:

- Title of the program and its location
- Name of evaluator(s)
- Name(s) of people to whom the evaluation report is to be submitted
- Period covered by the report
- Date the report is submitted

Make the front cover attractive, with carefully blocked formatting. The cover reflects your state of mind.

Section I. Summary

The summary is a brief overview of the evaluation report, explaining why
the evaluation was conducted and listing its major conclusions and recommendations. The summary is designed for people who are too busy to
read the full report and therefore it should be no more than one or two
pages long. Although the summary is placed first, it is the section that you
write last!

Typical Content

- What was evaluated?
- Why was the evaluation conducted?
- What are the major findings and recommendations of the evaluation?

And also, if space permits:

- Were there decisions to be made on the basis of the evaluation?
  If so, what decisions?
- To what audiences is the evaluation report addressed?
- Who else might find it interesting or important?
- What were the major constraints, if any, under which the evaluation
  had to be carried out?

Section II. Background Information Concerning the Program

This section sets the *program* in context. It describes how the program was
initiated and what it was supposed to do. The amount of detail presented
here will depend upon the audience and the people for whom the evaluation report is prepared. If the audience has no knowledge of the program,
it must be fully described. If, on the other hand, the evaluation report is
mainly intended for internal use and its readers are likely to be familiar
with the program, this section can be fairly brief, setting down information "for the record."

Regardless of the audience, if your report will be the sole lasting record
of the program to be recorded, then this section should contain consider-
able detail. This description of the program should be drafted *at the time
the evaluation is planned.* This will mean less work later, particularly at the
busy time when the data have been collected and must be analyzed. It will
also ensure for the evaluator, from the beginning, a clear grasp of the
program—its critical components and what they are supposed to accomplish. You should draft Section II, then, along with Section III, as soon as
possible after accepting the role of evaluator. Both sections should be
circulated to program personnel for comment.

Information helpful in writing this section can be gathered from myriad sources: a program plan or proposal, needs assessment reports, discussions with staff, PTA minutes, faculty meeting minutes, district memos, curriculum outlines, lists of goals, budget estimates, and so forth. The program director and staff probably have most of the information for this section in their heads, but reference to documents such as those listed will help you assess the consistency of their recollections with official program descriptions. It is important that you locate any *discrepancies* between recollections and program descriptions and resolve them before you write your report.

Typical Content

A. Origin of the program

- Where was the program implemented? What sort of communities? How many people—parents, teachers, students—did it affect? What special groups?
- In what *aggregate* did people participate? That is, is it more appropriate to talk about participants in terms of districts, schools, classrooms, or individuals?
- How did the program get started?
- Was a formal or informal *needs assessment* conducted, and if so, what were the results?
- Were there community, state, or national demands which led to the program? . . . or legal requirements? . . . or opportunities for funding? . . . or teacher initiatives? . . . or district requirements?

B. Goals of the program

- What was the program designed to accomplish?
- What goals or objectives were set? What was their order of priority, if any?

C. Students involved in the program

- For what age, grade level, ability level is the program appropriate?
- On what bases were students (or their classrooms, schools, districts) to be selected for the program?
- Were participants to remain in the program for its duration? If not, what criteria would determine the time of their entrance or exit?

D. Characteristics of the program materials, activities, and administrative arrangements

- What was the program supposed to look like? A table might describe this; see pages 50 and 54.

- What *materials* were to be used, and how? Were they to be custom-produced or purchased?
- What resources—funds, physical facilities, transportation—were to be available, and who was to provide them?
- In what *activities* were participants in the program, such as students, expected to take part?
- What specific procedures, if any, were teachers or other program implementors to follow?
- What is the rationale underlying the program? That is, why did the program's planners feel that the various program materials and activities would lead to the achievement of program goals?
- How highly prescribed was program implementation? How much was the program allowed to *vary* from site to site or from time to time?
- How was the program administered? What offices or roles were created or expanded? Who filled them? Did this represent a departure from usual practice?
- To what extent does this section describe the program as it was *supposed* to look as opposed to how it *did* look? Will the *Results* section (IVB) of the report contain backup data scrutinizing the accuracy of the program description reported here?

E. Faculty and others involved in the program

- How many teachers, administrators, consultants, secretaries, clerks, aides, volunteers, parents, and other adults were to be active in the program? What roles were they to assume?
- Were they required to have special training or credentials?
- Were any of these adults to *receive* training?
- How much time per week (day, month, year) were they to devote to the program?

Section III. Description of the Evaluation Study

The first part of this section describes and delimits the assignment that the evaluator has accepted. It explains *why* the evaluation was conducted, what it was intended to accomplish, and what it was *not* intended to accomplish. You should prepare the description of the purposes of the evaluation immediately after accepting the job as evaluator. A draft of this statement should be agreed upon by all interested parties and should be kept on file.

The remainder of this section describes the methodology of the evaluation—*how* the program was evaluated. It is important that this description be detailed; if people are to have faith in the conclusions of the evaluation, they need to know how the information was obtained. Samples of all instruments should be made available, with the exception of widely-used published tests or tests which by law may not be reproduced. Samples can be placed in an appendix, but it is helpful to the reader to have a few typical items reproduced in the body of the text.

As has been mentioned, Section III should be drafted when the evaluation is being planned; and it is a good idea to circulate a copy of this draft to program personnel. They are, after all, expected to cooperate with the evaluation and in some cases to act on its results. They should therefore understand how the evaluation is being conducted. If they are going to object to parts of the evaluation, then you should find this out early when necessary changes can be made, rather than later when the evaluation cannot be altered. You should elicit from the program staff agreement that your evaluation will provide a fair measure of their program.

Typical Content

Four major issues should be addressed:

A. Purposes of the evaluation

- Who requested the evaluation?
- Is it primarily formative or summative? That is, what was the evaluation required to do?
- If the evaluation was undertaken to enlighten a particular audience or audiences, who were they? The program staff? Parents? Community? The school board? State or federal agencies?
- What kind of information did the audience require?
- Was the evaluation undertaken to provide information needed for a decision? If so, what kind of decision? A decision might be a choice between two possible programs; or it might be a decision to continue, discontinue, or modify all or part of the program.
- Who were the decision makers, and what kind of information did they need from the evaluation study?
- Does the evaluation aim to answer correlational and/or research questions? If so, what are they?
- What was the context in which the evaluation was conducted? Were there restrictions, constraints on time or money, or other limitations placed on the study? Are there particular issues that the evaluator has agreed *not* to address?

B. Evaluation design(s)

- Did one basic evaluation design[3] underly all measurements made? What was it? If additional designs were used, what were they?
- Why were these particular designs chosen?
- What were the limitations of the designs used?
- What unavoidable confounds or contaminations were foreseen? What precautions were taken to avoid them? To what effect?
- Did certain circumstances prevent the use of more rigorous designs?

C. Outcome measures

Instruments used

- What program results—outcomes—were measured for the evaluation? Were these results mentioned among the program's goals, or have you chosen to measure them for some other reason?
- For each measurement, what data were collected? What instruments were used?
- Were the instruments developed in-house or were they purchased? If developed, how? If selected for purchasing, on what basis?
- How was instrument reliability assessed? Validity? Examinee appropriateness? Relevance to the program?

Data collection procedures

- What was the schedule for data collection? When were instruments administered, and who administered them? This is often best presented in a table, such as the one on page 52.
- Was training provided for those making various measurements? If so, how much and what kind of training?
- Was every student (or classroom, school, etc.) in every group measured, or were sampling procedures used?

D. Implementation measures

Instruments used

- Why was implementation described? To hold the program *accountable* for compliance to a proposal, plan, or philosophy of schooling? Or simply to *describe* what happened?

---

3. An evaluation *design* is a plan determining *when* evaluation instruments—tests, questionnaires, observations, record inspections, interviews, etc.—will be administered and *to whom*. Design provides a basis for *comparing* the results of measurements to a standard. This standard might be the performance of program participants prior to the program or the scores of a comparable group of *non*-participants.

- What crucial aspects of the program were observed, recorded, or otherwise measured? Why did you choose to focus on these features of implementation and not others?
- How were backup data collected to support your description of what the program looked like in operation? Informally, through reading program documents, observing, or conversing with staff? Or were more systematic data collection methods used?
- How were instruments, if any, developed? Were any ready-made ones borrowed or purchased? From whom, and on what basis?
- What limitations or deficiencies were there in the instruments?
- Were checks made on their reliability, validity, and appropriateness to the setting?

Data collection procedures

- What was the schedule for the collection of implementation information, and who collected it? A schedule is often well presented by a table.
- What training was provided, and what precautions were taken in the use of the instruments?
- Was a representative *sampling* of the program chosen for observation? Were instruments—questionnaires, interviews—administered to everyone or only some representative staff members?
- What limitations or deficiencies were there in the procedures used for measuring implementation?

Section IV. Results

This section presents the results of the various measurements, described in Section III, which were used to measure outcomes and program implementation. If the measurements were relevant, reliable, and valid, these results constitute *hard data* about the program. In addition, this section might also include some *soft data*—anecdotal evidence or testimonials about the program. Though soft data may not be regarded as conclusive because of their possible lack of representativeness, this kind of evidence enlivens the report and often gets across the program results that cannot be expressed as numbers. While a glowing letter from one parent does not show that the program was a success with all students, it may, however, communicate vividly some of the strengths of the program.

Before you begin to write the results section, all data should have been analyzed, recorded in tables, graphed or plotted, and tested for significance where appropriate. Scores from tests are usually presented in graphs and tables showing means and standard deviations for each group. Results of questionnaires are frequently summarized on a copy of the questionnaire itself.

If raw data were processed and analyzed in a large number of ways or using special procedures which need to be described or explained, then a section headed *Data Analysis Procedures* should be added between Sections III and IV. However, for most evaluations, data analysis can be presented in Section IV as the results from each instrument are reported.

Typical Content

Three issues should be addressed in this section:

A. Results of outcome measurements

- How many participants took pretests?
- How many of those who took pretests were still in the program group (or control group, if there was one) at the end of the program? Was there a difference in the percentage of participants leaving the program and control groups over the program's duration? Use an attrition table, page 53, to summarize this.
- What were the results of pretests? Was there a difference in pretest scores among program and comparison groups?
- For *each measurement* made, what were the posttest—or midtest— results for participants in the program and for participants in the comparison groups? How do they compare? Are differences statistically significant? What table or graph best summarizes this? See Chapter 4.
- If there was no control group, how much did program group performance change from test to test?
- If there was no control group, to what can results be compared in order to judge their quality? For example, test norms, past performance at program sites, or standards set to reflect different levels of competence may be used for such purposes of comparison. Can comparisons be shown graphically? See pages 12, 63, 75, and 76.
- What were the results of statistical tests designed to answer questions about correlations among participants or program characteristics? See page 57 for a discussion of graphs and tables for expressing correlations.

B. Results of implementation measurements

- Did the staff deliver the program they had promised?
- Was the program implemented as planned and as the audience expected? If not, what happened? Were some components dropped or modified? Were all materials available, and were they used? Was the program given to the students for whom it was planned? Did crucial activities in fact occur?

- What (in as much detail as possible) did the program finally look like? Will a table describe this well? See pages 50 and 54.
- If changes occurred in the program, what effects did they have on, for instance, staff and student attitudes or efficiency of operation?
- How similar was the program from site to site? What variations were allowed?
- What did a typical lesson or program experience look like?

C. **Informal results**

- Are there available informal comments or narrative summaries of reports which illustrate the findings indicated by the hard data? These might be anecdotal accounts from teachers, parent letters, questionnaire responses, student essays, or transcripts of informal observations by principals.
- Were these testimonials about the program solicited or voluntary?

Section V. Discussion of Results

Interpretation of each result could occur in Section IV where it is presented. However, if the program and/or the evaluation is complicated, a separate section for interpreting and discussing the results makes the report clearer. The results should be discussed with particular reference to the Purposes of the Evaluation listed in Section IIIA.

Typical Content

There are two major issues to be addressed in this section:

A. **How certain is it that the program caused the results?**

- Are there alternative explanations of program results? For example, were the gains made by students perhaps simply the result of normal maturation? Were there confounds that need to be considered? If there was a control group, was there any contamination? Attempt here to anticipate and answer arguments against your attribution of program results that might be raised by a skeptic.

B. **How good were the results of the program?**

- How did the program results compare with what might have been expected had there been no program?
- If a control group was used, were the program results better than control group results? If the difference was statistically significant, was the size or quality of the difference enough to make it educationally significant? If the difference was not statistically significant, did program results appear promising at least?

- If there was no control group, how do results compare with whatever standard for judging their quality has been established?
- Does the staff feel the program would achieve more significant gains were it to be modified or run for a longer period of time? Is there evidence in your data to support this point of view?
- What conclusions or recommendations can be made from correlational studies? Do certain program features, for example, seem most effective with certain groups? Are attitudes or achievement related to student, teacher, or parent characteristics?

Section VI. Costs and Benefits (optional)

This section takes a close look at the program budget—an area fraught with controversy. Since there is as yet no well-reputed way to collect, analyze, or present cost-benefit information, this section will be devoted to two things:

1. Justifying the usefulness of the particular approach to cost-benefit analysis you have taken.
2. Presenting and interpreting your data.[4]

A cost-benefit discussion essentially lists the dollar costs associated with the program and then broadens into a summary of other non-dollar, qualitative costs. The benefits of the program are then described and weighed against these costs.

If possible, provide in this section a *table* in which costs and benefits are listed.

Typical Content

Three major issues to be considered are:

A. Your method for calculating costs and benefits

- How have you defined *Costs? Benefits*?
- What method have you used to compute costs and benefits? Is it a formal mathematical one, perhaps involving equations? Or does it rely on informal methods of contrasting costs and benefits? What precedents can you cite for use of this method? Where has it been used to good result in the past?

---

4. If costs and benefits are a major focus of your evaluation, you might want to include cost and benefit data in the *Results* section, with discussion integrated into Section V.

B. Costs associated with the program

Dollar costs

- What extra monies were required to implement the program? What was the source of these?
- What would the money have been used for had it not been used in the program?
- What portion of the money spent on the program represents operating costs; what were the program's *start-up* costs? The latter will not be needed if the program is continued. A table showing program dollar expenses should be included.

Non-dollar costs

- Did the program take a toll on teacher, parent, student, or administrator patience, morale, etc?
- Did teachers or others work overtime because of the program?
- Were there volunteers whose time was used by the program? If so, what would they have been doing had they not been working in the program?
- Did participation in the program deprive students of other valuable experiences?
- What other costs did the program produce either through bad morale or by using up resources or causing the loss of alternative opportunities?

C. Benefits associated with the program

Dollar benefits

- What financial income was received in support of or as a result of the program? For example, did the state reimburse the district for a special education program?

Non-dollar benefits

- For what positive results do you have evidence?
- How much progress was made toward program goals?
- Were outcomes for students in the program significantly better than for similar students not in the program?
- How big a difference did the program make?
- How much was the program valued by various groups?
- Were there any unanticipated benefits due to the program at the program site or in the broader community?

Section VII. Conclusions and Recommendations

It is best to present this section in the form of a list rather than as a narrative. The recommendations can be the most influential part of the evaluation report. Be sure, therefore, to emphasize what is important, and to make clear which conclusions must be *tentatively* rather than *firmly* drawn. Take care that this section attends to all the concerns that were described in detail in Section IIIA, your description of the Purpose of the Evaluation.

Typical Content

The three major entries for this section are:

A. Conclusions

- What are the major conclusions to be drawn about the effectiveness of the program as a whole? Of its various subcomponents? How firm are these conclusions?
- Must judgment be withheld regarding some aspects of the program?
- Did the evaluation overlook features or effects of the program that should have been considered in order to provide a complete picture of its impact?

B. Recommendations regarding the program

- On the basis of the evaluation, what recommendations can you make concerning the program?
- What predictions, hypotheses, or hunches are suggested by the results? What recommendations about further programs or research studies can be made?

C. Recommendations concerning subsequent evaluations of the program

- What instruments served their purpose well and would therefore be recommended for use in subsequent evaluations of this or similar programs?
- Should some instruments or evaluation procedures be modified or discarded for subsequent evaluations?
- Should components of the overall program be separately evaluated?
- If this evaluation has not been able to provide firm answers to some questions raised about the program, what evaluation design could yield such answers?

Chapter 3

Communicating
Evaluation Information:
Some Practical Tips[5]

Whether or not you are required to produce a lengthy, technical evaluation report, you undoubtedly have responsibility for *distributing* the results of the evaluation to the various audiences concerned. This chapter provides you with some practical tips that have helped other evaluators distribute their information effectively.

The chapter covers 18 tips in all, organized into the following categories:

- About evaluation audiences
- About the evaluation message
- About the written medium
- About verbal presentations
- About difficult audiences
- About working with the press

Some of these tips may sound rather "political." They are. *There is no such thing as an evaluation free from political considerations.* Some of the tips may seem obvious to you, based on commonly accepted principles. The chapter includes this fairly standard advice not because you have not heard it before, but in the interest of completeness. It is hoped that you will use the time spent reading this chapter to examine your particular reporting task and to think about how and what you will report.

---

5. This chapter was assembled by two practicing evaluators, Ann Moore Lee and Freda M. Holley, in the course of their employment in the research and evaluation office of the Austin, Texas, Independent School District.

About Evaluation Audiences

The composition and needs of the evaluation audience probably account for the most critical and complex problems facing the evaluator. Fraught with political ramifications, the desires of the evaluation's audience should be seriously examined both at the beginning of the evaluation and throughout the evaluation process. Long before the preparation of any report, the following key questions, at minimum, should already have been answered:

• Who needs to know? Which groups? Which key people?
• What information is to be provided? In what sequence? In what form? When?
• What problems are likely to occur in giving information to these particular people and groups?

Your evaluation plan should evolve with these answers in mind. Tips 1, 2, and 3 are about evaluation audiences and the ways in which you could err in working with them.

1. Know your audiences

Most evaluations have many audiences. Neglecting to correctly identify one or more of them is a common mistake, and an ignored audience can cause problems. Try to avoid problems like these:

a. Say, for example, that you have conducted for a small district an ESEA Title I evaluation, collecting and reporting the information required by the State Department of Education. You report the results of the evaluation to everyone in the district at a meeting at the end of the school year. To your dismay *parents* become instantly upset. They had no voice in planning the evaluation. It does not reflect *local* concerns, they say. The Parent Advisory Committee, therefore, refuses to even hear, let alone support, your recommendations for next year's program. By overlooking them at a critical stage, and undervaluing their importance as an evaluation audience, you may have alienated a local group, possibly the one most in a position to derive something useful from your results.

b. An error as serious as *overlooking* an audience is failure to submit the report in time to help the audience make a decision. Perhaps, for example, you find that teachers are displeased with a set of program materials. They have discovered through use that audiovisual materials they initially liked are too complex to use, an outcome which you include in your report at the end of the year. This has not been in time, however, to prevent the principal from purchasing several additional sets of materials based on the early favorable reports. Here, an audience made a decision in ignorance of vital information. This problem may be unavoidable when decisions need to be made either under crisis or in ad hoc situations. It *can* be avoided if you know, in advance, *who* will be deciding *what*—and *when*.

c. Another potential problem is identification of too broad or too narrow an audience. Perhaps, for instance, you have addressed your report to a program planning committee when actually your audience should have been the committee chairperson. She is the respected opinion leader of the group. She always determines the committee's actions on any issue. A wiser focus for your report, then, will be toward informing and persuading this one influential person of the soundness and possible implications of the evaluation information. On the other hand, you may find that within such a committee there are several people with strong opinions who need convincing.

Identifying your actual audiences—sometimes in spite of official pronouncements—is critical if you hope that your findings will do something more than occupy space in a filing cabinet.

2. Find out what information they need and, if possible, why they need it

Producing a list of what people want to know—and why—can be a harrowing but educational experience for a variety of reasons:

- Different audiences want different information—even to answer the same question.
- Some audiences do not know what they need.
- Some audiences will be quite certain and even candid about what they need *because they have an ax to grind.* That is, they want the evaluation to support a particular point of view.

If you want the audience to listen carefully when you begin circulating your findings, you will have to pay attention to what they want to know. An audience of teachers, primed to find out about teaching strategies that seem to be most effective with low income students, will not be interested in a report on teacher attitudes *unless the connection between strategies and attitudes is clearly demonstrated.* A group of parents who have been insisting that their children be better prepared to enter the job market after high school graduation will not be satisfied with the report that the number of students going on to college has risen by 15%.

Be careful to avoid giving decision makers almost but not quite what they need to know. The superintendent, for example, might need to know approximately how many teachers will voluntarily agree to accept transfers when the district's desegregation plan goes into effect. You cannot respond to this with information about the number of teachers who *endorse* voluntary teacher transfers. Endorsing teacher transfers is not quite the same as volunteering to transfer oneself.

It often happens, as well, that an audience's information needs change while an evaluation is in progress. Some parents, for example, might mention that although students seem to be learning in the math program, they have developed a strong antipathy to math. If your evaluation plan does not include attitude measures, this new information might indicate that it should. Although you cannot constantly alter evaluation plans to meet changing needs, try to reserve some small portion of your resources to meet requirements for ad hoc information that crops up during program implementation.

3. Try to understand each audience's viewpoint

To understand an audience's viewpoint, you must know its idiosyncracies and the reasons why it acts as it does. This understanding is especially important in order to anticipate the kinds of situations that will trigger negative reactions.

Teachers frequently complain—with just cause—about being required to attend meetings on topics in which they have no interest. Many teachers, in addition, have developed negative attitudes toward decisions made at "the central office" by "all those desk jockeys up there who have nothing better to do than dream up more paperwork for us." If you plan to report evaluation information to teachers whom you know hold these attitudes, you should plan your reporting strategy around the following:

Attitude	Possibilities for Adjusting Reporting to Accommodate to the Attitude
I don't want to go to another meeting that eats into my sparse planning time.	• Distribute the information in a memo or a brochure. • Post the information on a bulletin board in the faculty lounge. • Provide the information quickly during a regularly scheduled faculty meeting. • Meet with one teacher per grade and let these teachers tell the others. • Ask the principal or teachers to decide on the most convenient time for a meeting.
I don't like the central office.	• Have the principal or some teachers present the information to their colleagues. • Present the information jointly with the principal or a teacher. • Pay attention to what you wear. Dress as you expect your audience will dress.

About the Evaluation Message

The next two tips help prescribe the *form* of the message you relay to your audience.

4. Relate the information to action which must be taken

In most evaluation reports, especially more formal ones, the decisions or concerns which the evaluation addresses, if they are mentioned at all, are reported in a different section from the evaluation results. Notice that in Chapter 2, Section IIIA, the formal report outline calls for a discussion of the *decisions* to be made from the evaluation findings. Description of the *results* of the evaluation is delayed until Section V, parts A and B. In the logical progression of the report, the results are removed from the decision questions. They need not be, however, and in most situations you might wish to get these two items as close to each other as possible. One way to do this—though not the only one—is to list each decision question and immediately afterwards summarize the evaluation findings which relate to it. This technique provides the busy reader with a quick summary of all the available information about the decision area. Figure 3, page 32, presents an example of this idea.

You do not, of course, always have to *recommend a course of action* in your report, although making such recommendations may be appropriate in some cases, particularly in a formative evaluation.

5. Do not give the audience more than it needs

If you expect the audience to accurately absorb the information it most needs, do not confuse things by overwhelming it with other interesting but not necessarily vital information. If a principal asks you in a meeting what a standard deviation means, do not make the mistake of covering the blackboard with statistical equations and graphs. This one indiscretion could destroy all you have worked for up to that point. When you give an audience too much, *all* of your information becomes confusing.

Violating this rule is particularly easy when you must address a prestigious group, say for example, a school board. For one thing, you probably were taught early in life that people in high authority should be told everything. For another, you have probably devoted a chunk of your life to the evaluation project, fending off dangers to the evaluation plan, and working long hours. You are eager, perhaps, to show the audience the clarity and brilliant complexity of the evaluation plan, the quick-thinking administrative maneuvers that saved the evaluation from disaster, or the mathematical genius so obviously guiding the analyses. DO NOT DO IT! You will bore the audience to death and render the report indigestible.

Decision Question

Should the district provide a fourth (summer) quarter for students
in grades 7-12?

Information Summary

11% of the secondary students are interested in attending an additional fourth quarter, and 18% of the teachers are willing to teach
an additional fourth quarter.

All secondary students were surveyed about their reasons for wanting
to attend a fourth summer quarter. The results:

Reasons given by students who said they would attend a summer quarter:	Grades				
	7	8	9	10	11
For enrichment	26%	20%	19%	18%	27%
To graduate early	29%	22%	32%	45%	60%
To catch up	43%	57%	48%	34%	12%
Other	2%	1%	1%	3%	1%

All secondary teachers in the district were surveyed to assess their
availability for teaching the fourth summer quarter. The results:

 18% - would teach all four quarters

 45% - could teach summer quarter if they could get off another
       quarter

 33% - not available to teach a summer quarter under any circum-
       stances

  4% - want more information

100%

Figure 3. An example from an evaluation report of a
format for relating evaluation information to an
action which must be taken

Most evaluation reports released to a lay audience err by including more
than is needed. Of course, many situations will require that you describe
both the program and the evaluation in a *technical report* to be submitted
to audiences who need this information.

About the Written Medium

This section deals especially with *written* efforts to communicate evaluation information. The principles in this section apply to memos, news releases, and written communications other than formal evaluation reports. They can be applied, as well, to formal and informal oral presentations.

6. Start with the most important information

When reading for information, readers seek out the most important points first. Having learned these larger "truths," they then have a skeleton on which to hang the smaller, less significant pieces of the message. This principle underlines the familiar, though vital, advice:
> "Tell them what you're going to tell them, then tell them, then tell them what you told them."

Evaluation reports which follow the standard outline sound like college dissertations. This loyalty to prespecified scientific formats stems, no doubt, partly from evaluators' desires to be accepted as genuine researchers. Although a dissertation outline has many merits, it does not provide the reader with what he wants to know *when* he wants to know it.

David Ewing[6] recommends that a piece of professional writing should meet five requirements:

1. Does the opening paragraph or section specify the *subject matter* of the report, memorandum, letter, or other document?
2. Does the opening telegraph the principal *message* that the writer will emphasize?
3. If it is important to the reader to know *why* the document was written, is the reason made clear?
4. If the report is lengthy or complex, does the opening section outline the *organizational scheme* to be followed?
5. If the report were to be sent out with a covering letter for some reason, would you be able to forego summarizing in the letter the main ideas, conclusions, or recommendations of the report?

A good way to ensure conciseness is to *imagine that your reader will not have time to get through the whole report.* Plan that some interruption may cause the report to be laid aside and perhaps never be looked at again. You have to say as much as possible right away!

Here are some more specific suggestions for providing the reader with easy access to the salient parts in the report:

---

6. Ewing, D. W. *Writing for results in business, government, and the professions.* New York: John Wiley and Sons, 1974 (59-62).

- Put a clear abstract at the front.
- Make your *Evaluation Findings* the first chapter.
- Start *each* chapter, subsection, and paragraph of your report with the most important point to be made in that section. Put your diamonds right on top of the heap to be sure they will be seen by your readers.

7. Highlight the important points

Help your reader determine what facts are most important. Obviously, putting the most important information first is one way, but there are additional ways to do this:

a. Use *descriptive section headings*. For example, the heading *Teacher Attitudes* tells you less than *Teacher Attitudes Toward the Program* which tells you less than *Teachers Favor the Program*. Headings in a report serve the same function as headlines in a newspaper. Descriptive section headings can also spark interest and motivate the reader to read further. Interesting and informative headings will pull a reader through a report that would not otherwise be read to its conclusion.

b. Write the first draft of your report using as many section headings as you can think of; then read it over and double the number of headings.

c. Try using headings as a running commentary, parallel to the report text:

CLOVERDALE   The "average Cloverdale first-
FIRST-GRADERS   grader" comes to school only
ON PAR WITH   slightly less well-prepared to
NATIONAL   start his academic career than
AVERAGE   does the "average American first-
                    grader." The districtwide pre-
                    reading readiness score was at
                    the 48th percentile.

d. The *spacing and layout* of a report text can be used to highlight information. Consider this text:

The three areas of the district show rather different patterns of strengths and weaknesses on the
subtests. For South Side and North Hills students,
Math Concepts is the weakest subtest and Math Computation the strongest, with Reading in between.

For Central City students, on the other hand, all
reading scores are higher than the math scores, and
there is no difference between the two math subtests.
North Hills students tend to score higher than South
Side students in math, but about the same in reading.

Reformatting improves its readability:

Addition of an outline format, with dots and more white space	The three areas of the district show somewhat different patterns of strengths and weaknesses on the subtests:

· For South Side and North Hills students,
  Math Concepts is the weakest subtest and
  Math Computation the strongest, with
  Reading in between.

· For Central City students, on the other
  hand, all reading scores are higher than
  the math scores, and there is no difference between the two math subtests.

· North Hills students tend to score
  higher than South Side students in math,
  but about the same in reading.

Boxes

> For South Side and North Hills students,
> Math Concepts is the weakest subtest and
> Math Computation the strongest, with
> Reading in between.

Changes in
typestyle

For *Central City* students, on the other
hand, all reading scores are higher than
the math scores, and there is no difference between the two math subtests.

Underlining

<u>North Hills</u> students tend to score higher
than South Side students in math, but
about the same in reading.

Capital letters	For SOUTH SIDE and NORTH HILLS students, Math Concepts is the weakest subtest and Math Computation the strongest, with reading in between.

8. Make your report readable

Whether your audience consists of professionals or laymen, its members are busy people. You should therefore make the reading easy without sacrificing accuracy. Consider these pointers to help increase reading ease:

a. Before you start to write, create an imaginary reader. Assume that this reader is the parent of a student and not a professional educator. As you write, keep this person in mind.

b. If you feel suitably uninhibited, dictate the first draft into a tape recorder. Again, imagine that you are explaining the various aspects of the program to an interested, but relatively uninformed individual.

c. Once you have a draft, check the vocabulary to make sure you have used familiar words.

Instead of:	Use:
obfuscate	cloud
configuration	pattern
differential	gap
dichotomous cross-classification	2 x 2 table
utilize	use
facilitate	help

Jargon, a shorthand language that develops among specialists, is not easily understood by outsiders. Most jargon, while adding words to the language, does little to improve it. Ernest Boyer, U.S. Commissioner of Education, once complained that a manuscript was too technical for release to the general public. When the criticism was voiced to a colleague, the reply was, "I guess we'll have to laymanize it"![7]

If you must use a technical term unfamiliar to readers, define it clearly. This may be done in a footnote, an aside, or as part of a glossary, if the report must contain *several* technical terms. The importance of defining words that are likely to be unfamiliar to your reader cannot be overstressed.

---

7. Cited by George Neill in "Washington Report." *Phi Delta Kappan, 59*(7), March, 1978.

d. Use active verbs as much as possible. Generally, active verbs shorten sentences and increase their impact.

Example

Passive verb sentence: The scores of the children in the program were higher than those of the children in the control group. (19 words)

Active verb sentence: Children in the program scored higher than children in the control group. (12 words)

---

e. Cut out the deadwood. As you edit your report, look for unnecessary words and phrases. Sometimes editing is best done by someone else. If you must do it yourself, allow a day or two to pass between when you write and when you edit.

f. Shorten your sentences. Cutting out deadwood and using active verbs will shorten some of your sentences. Others that are still too long should be broken apart.

Example

The community advisory group held informative as well as entertaining monthly programs at different project schools during September through June, but did not meet in December. (26 words)

The community advisory group held informative and entertaining monthly meetings at different project schools. They met every month between September and June, except December. (24 words)

---

g. Write shorter paragraphs. There is nothing so discouraging as looking at a solid wall of text. As you edit your material, try to convert these solid walls to shorter paragraphs. Ideas which require lengthy discussion, of course, are not easily broken down. But where you can confine paragraphs to a single idea, you will increase readers' understanding of the material and reduce the effort they must expend.

Even one-sentence paragraphs can be very effective.

h. Personalize your text. Try to make your text sound less like an insurance policy and more like a letter to a friend. Of course, you must judge whether or not this tip is appropriate to your audience(s). Some audiences will respond well to a casual, personal approach; others will expect and want a formal document. Here are ways you can personalize the material:

Use first person pronouns. Until recently, the use of *I* and *we* in writing was considered improper. The current fashion is such that referring to yourself and your audience as *he* and *they* often sounds stilted and false.

Use contractions. Contractions in written text tend to make the material more natural. They're being used more and more in "formal" written material—even in annual reports for business and industry.

Use "shirtsleeves" language. As you rack your brains for a way to say that a program component is headed for hard times unless changes are made immediately, consider saying it this way: "The program component is headed for hard times unless changes are made immediately." If your audience does not mind the informality, it will certainly understand your message. Ewing[8] reports that phrases like "pull the rug out from under us" and "catcalls from the sidelines" have been found in technical reports to the President of the United States. Casual but expressive shirtsleeves terms can be quite effective, but only *when used sparingly*.

About Verbal Presentations

Practicing evaluators have discovered a few principles to increase success when making verbal presentations to evaluation audiences. These are summarized in tips 9 through 12.

9. Make the presentation interesting and varied

A verbal presentation should have enough variety to keep the audience entertained. Only an awake audience can be expected to hear your message. Almost anything you can do to get and keep their attention is therefore warranted. The positive reception given to even slightly interesting evaluation presentations reflects the deadly, dull character that audiences expect such presentations to have.

Here are some techniques for adding interest to your oral reports:

a. Do something different. This means something different from what the audience is used to. The lecture approach is the most common method of presentation. Audiences expecting a lecture will perk up at the appearance of half-a-dozen slides or transparencies. Some examples of novel presentation formats include, but are certainly not limited to:

---

8. Ewing, D. W. *Writing for results in business, government, and the professions.* New York: John Wiley and Sons, 1974.

- Skits—do not rule this out; it can work well with many evaluation topics
- Audiovisual shows with commentary
- Symposia or panel discussions involving the program's major actors
- Question and answer sessions

b. Vary the format. Five minutes of lecture, four minutes of lecture with slides, one minute of slides with no commentary, four minutes of questions and answers, and one final minute of lecture summary—this scenario probably makes a more interesting showing than fifteen straight minutes of lecture only. You can provide variety in many ways. Visuals, for example, can include any or all of the following: numbers, quotations, cartoons and drawings, photographs, and graphs. Try having two or more presenters. Perhaps they could argue or present opposing interpretations of the evaluation report. For the sake of sheer movement, try shifting the focus of the presentation to different parts of the room.

10. Do what comes naturally

It is important that you deliver a smooth, practiced, confident presentation. While a little nervousness won't hurt anything, if you are too shaky, your audience's attention will focus on you and not your message. You will feel least nervous with the presentation style that is most natural to you, regardless of whatever else has been said in this chapter. Many people, for instance, find it easier to talk to groups when there is something else to do besides just talk, such as show visuals or operate equipment. Knowing people in the audience also helps to relieve stage fright. However, when you must give a presentation to strangers, find out something about them that will help you see them as similar to people you have successfully talked with in the past.

Practice can certainly improve your presentation. Perhaps some friends could critique your delivery. Complicated audiovisual presentations will need several dry runs with attention given to the arrangement of the equipment and the room. If you fear a question and answer session, have friends or colleagues ask you the most difficult questions they can think of and then critique your answers. A word of caution here: If you do begin with this kind of practice, you must continue it until you feel comfortable. A *little* practice can sometimes *heighten* anxiety.

11. Make the visuals large and simple

Visuals which accompany verbal presentations must be large enough for the audience to see. You would be surprised how many speakers violate this rule. When designing a visual, find out where the person farthest from the visual will be sitting, and design the visual so that she can see it clearly. Charts full of numbers, unless they are very large (wall-size), are not effective with large groups, though they can be used with presentations to just a few people. Even then, though, the charts must be large enough so that people sitting several feet away can see them.

Do not make transparencies for the overhead projector from typed material unless you use a typewriter with very large type, perhaps a primary typewriter. You *can,* however, use typewritten copy—especially from a 10-pitch (pica) or a primary typewriter—to make slides. Remember not to put too many words on the slide; one to ten words is sufficient. Most slides used to support oral presentations contain too much information; the audience is not allowed sufficient time to think about what it is seeing.

12. Involve the audience in the presentation

Find a way to have your audience act or respond during the presentation. Learner involvement with the material is a basic teaching principle. Involving an audience can be as subtle as getting them to laugh at opening jokes or as overt as having them roleplay. You could, for example, ask teachers to roleplay presentation of your achievement test results to parents with whom they will be conferencing.

Here are a few audience involvement techniques:

- Ask for a show of hands in answer to questions; for example, "How many of you have worked in schools?" This also helps you better identify your audience's background.
- Ask them to predict results before you present them.
- Ask members of the audience to group themselves into particular seating arrangements.
- Ask them to help interpret your results. You might even ask for suggestions about how to present your *written* report.
- Build audience activities into your presentation. For example, give out cards on which people can write questions to be answered after your formal presentation; or arrange for group discussions about sections of your report.
- Ask the audience to take notes on the presentation instead of preparing handouts to be taken home. Or have them fill in blanks you have left in the handouts to emphasize what you want them to particularly notice.
- Test them on the material you have presented. This can be safely done more frequently than you think.
- Ask someone in the audience for help with the equipment.

One last tip: Do not apologize for involving an audience in your presentation. If you are apologetic or give the impression you are impinging on their rights, they may feel that indeed you are. People won't mind participating if you seem to know what you are doing.

About Difficult Audiences

Audiences may at one time or another be difficult—slow to comprehend, skeptical, or even hostile. Since standard methods of presentation are often inadequate in adversity, the following tips are offered:

13. Have the audience teach the content of the report to someone else

This principle, well applied, might consist of:

- Having a principal present, or co-present with you, the evaluation findings to teachers.
- Having the program director report the evaluation findings to the program officer.
- Having the teachers present the evaluation findings to the parents.

You could, in fact, arrange that evaluation results be distributed from group to group along the official chain of command in the district. Figure 4 shows the flow of shared evaluation results within a school district. This arrangement forces each district staff member to look at the evaluation results at least twice: upon receiving them and when passing them on.

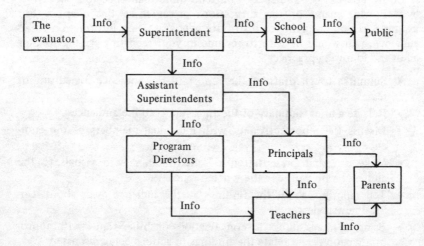

Figure 4. The flow of evaluation information along the chain of command in a school district

This approach is only effective, of course, if information is delivered accurately at the lower levels. If you choose this approach, you will probably need to deliver training and monitor the communications system.

14. Have someone else deliver the information

Try to be realistic about when you can and cannot handle distributing evaluation results yourself. Perhaps you:

- Lack direct access to the audience
- Are short on skills needed to effectively get across the information; for example, maybe you have stage fright
- Are immersed in a personality or ideological conflict with members of the audience

In such situations, find someone without these disadvantages to deliver the information. Remember, your main objective is to get the audience to understand and use the evaluation information.

15. Reinforce, reinforce, reinforce

A common problem with reporting evaluation information is that the audience usually hears it only once. To be properly absorbed, it should be heard more .often than that. It should be reinforced. You cannot, after all, blame audiences for not using evaluation information if they never understood it. You can get audiences to attend more than once to your report by following many of the suggestions presented in this chapter. For example, if you are going to distribute new evaluation information to an audience, you would be wise to include in your reporting strategy one or all of the following practices:

- Submit a rough draft of the report to the audience for editing or review.
- Release a brief summary of the final report to the audience.
- Discuss the report privately with individual members of the audience.
- Make a verbal presentation of the findings with visuals to the audience who will read the written report.
- Tell reporters about the findings so the audience reads about it in local newspapers.
- Bring up the findings in conversations on other topics with appropriate people, and relate the findings to actions being discussed.
- Have the audience present the information to other audiences.

About Working With the Press

Tips 16 through 18 give some advice about making reporters' jobs easier and ushering your evaluation through the public media so that it is reported accurately. Note that some of these suggestions could be applied to any audience.

16. Train reporters

Most reporters assigned to education beats have not had sufficient training to easily understand statistical evaluation studies.[9] Their generally high intelligence coupled with native curiosity, though, makes them good and grateful recipients of in-service training. You can educate reporters by means of formal workshops or one-to-one discussions.

Formal training workshops should not be propaganda sessions. They should deal strictly with concepts the reporters need to understand to easily and correctly interpret the sorts of evaluation information you distribute. These sessions will be better attended and more effective if they are held just prior to the release of some important information. You might even go so far as to hold a training session for reporters during the hour or so before the press conference begins. Consider, for instance, the value of discussing, immediately prior to releasing standardized test scores, such topics as these:

- What are percentile scores?
- How are percentile scores derived?
- What is wrong with the statement, "All children should be able to read at grade level"?
- What are some well-known correlates of achievement test scores?

When you consider the number of people, including school personnel, who get their information from newspapers, radio, and television, you realize how much confusion can be avoided by an information workshop.

Take advantage, as well, of every opportunity you find to give one-to-one training. Reporters who want a story badly will generally listen to anything in order to get it. Interviews, then, can be a fruitful setting for some teaching by you and learning by them. Assume, when being inter-

---

9. An evaluator once administered the Sequential Tests of Educational Progress (a high school achievement norm-referenced test) to a local newspaper reporter at his request. The 12th grade norms were used to derive his scores. This very successful, talented young newspaperman (with a B.A. in social studies) scored in the *90th+* percentiles on the English, writing, and social studies subtests, and at the *1st* percentile on the math concepts subtest!

viewed, that the reporter knows nothing about the topic you are discussing. Explain your jargon, and give mini-courses on things like:

- The benefits and difficulties of random assignment of subjects to control groups
- Significance tests—what they mean
- Criterion- and norm-referenced tests—their benefits and limitations

You may see the results of these conversations reflected in clearer news articles or feature articles about non-crisis, non-sensational aspects of evaluation or education. The best benefit these discussions can have is development of mutual respect between you and the press. Cooperative relations can only improve the accuracy and thoroughness of the evaluation news that the public receives.

17. Write news releases

Misquoting by reporters is common, usually because a reporter did not record the comment correctly in the first place or because he or she did not have time to write it down and was forced to reconstruct the comment from memory. You can guard against this situation by writing *news releases* and giving them to reporters before a press conference or interview. News releases should be clear, to-the-point, and comprehensive. Well-written news releases will cause a reporter's "quote-accuracy index" to go up and your blood pressure to come down.

News releases should follow most of the rules presented above under tips 6 to 8, "About the Written Medium." The best tip to remember is number 6—put the most important information at the beginning of the article. *Quotations* are good ways to draw attention to the most important points within a news release. For example:

> Superintendent John Jefferson said today, "An evaluation study shows that our students learn more after they enroll in Project-Excell than they were learning before they enrolled."

A news release should include the name, address, and phone numbers—work and home—of the person who should be contacted in case of confusion or if the reporter needs more information. If the news must be published on a certain day or will be outdated after a certain time, this should also be prominently mentioned. The news release should close with the marks ### to let the reporter or editor know that he has come to the end of the news release, not just the bottom of the first page.

Your district's public relations officer may be the appropriate person to send out the news release. Be sure to check policy before doing this on your own. Figure 5 is an example of a news release.

```
                              NEWS RELEASE

Contact:    Dr. Ruth Pitts                           May 2, 1979
            Director, Research & Evaluation          (Release on
            Passell School District                 May 5, 1979)
            145 Oak Avenue
            Passell, Texas

Phone #:    (512) 413-1045 (work)
            (512) 825-4711 (home)


        "Passell students scored higher this year on their annual
    achievement tests than they did last year."  Superintendent John
    Jefferson made this announcement in a special news conference.

        High school and junior high students scored an average of two to
    three percentile points higher than last year, and elementary stu-
    dents scored three to five percentile points higher.

        "We can't be sure exactly why our students are doing better,"
    Jefferson said.  "But we think that the increase is related to the
    changes we have made in our reading and math courses."

        For the past year, teachers and curriculum specialists in the
    district have been revising the math and reading courses.  These
    revisions were requested by the School Board in April, 1978, in
    response to parents' concerns about reading and math achievement.

        Jefferson offered another explanation for the improved scores.
    "During the last few years, students and teachers may not have been
    taking the test as seriously as we think it deserves to be taken.
    This year, however, attendance on the test days was higher than it's
    been during the past five years," he said.

        Dr. Ruth Pitts, director of research for the district, added,
    "Our research staff monitored the testing.  We made unannounced
    visits to five percent of the classes when the testing occurred and
    found that correct testing procedures were followed closely."

        Students will receive their individual scores at the end of May
    in brochures that explain the scores.  Students are being asked to
    take the brochures home to their parents.

        The tests were given to students during the middle of April.
    High school students took the Sequential Tests of Educational Prog-
    ress (reading, writing, math, science, and social studies).  Elemen-
    tary and junior high students took the California Achievement Tests
    (reading and mathematics).

                                 ###
```

Figure 5. Example of a news release

18. Be honest with reporters

You must consciously strive to achieve a reputation for credibility and
straightforwardness with all your audiences. A person whose job is to

collect and share information cannot be caught dissembling or lying. This is particularly true when talking to reporters. You should answer reporters' questions honestly. If you cannot do so, tell them clearly why you cannot. For example:

> "The administration and school board are studying the report right now. It would be a violation of my contract with them to discuss the report with the press before they have had a chance to review it. The superintendent will release the report to the public and the press in a week. I will be glad to answer any questions that you might have then."

Such candor will be accepted, even if reluctantly.

Many times reporters ask seemingly simple questions to which they want simple answers: "Why do minorities score lower on achievement tests than whites?" or "Why isn't Program X succeeding?" Your immediate desire might be to preface answers to these questions with hours of background. If possible, condense those hours of explanation into a five minute summary. Your summary should give the reporter some feel for the complexity of the situation. If the question is one to which you do not know the answer or if you are not familiar with the research in the area, do not bluff. You are likely to find your weak generalities printed on page one of the local paper.

You must accept that reporters are talking to you for only one reason—to get a story. To write a story that sells, they must ask hard questions. Their who, what, where, and when questions are easy to answer—they are the same questions you answered in the evaluation:

- *Who* is the program serving?
- *What* are the program effects?

Reporters will insistently ask *why* questions. These, of course, will likely have complex answers. In response to all their questions, easy or hard, you must give honest answers phrased in a way that the reporters understand.

In summary, being honest with reporters means:

- Being open and honest when responding to questions
- Trying not to mislead them with a simplistic description of a complex situation
- Refusing to bluff reporters or fake answers to their questions—doing this can backfire disastrously

For Further Reading

Ewing, D. W. *Writing for results in business, government, and the professions.* New York: John Wiley and Sons, 1974.

Flesch, R. *The art of plain talk.* New York: Harper and Brothers, 1946.

Flesch, R. *The art of readable writing.* New York: Harper and Brothers, 1949.

National School Public Relations Association. *Releasing test scores: Educational assessment programs, How to tell the public.* Arlington, VA: Author, 1976. (Available from National School Public Relations Association, 1801 North Moore Street, Arlington, VA 22209.)

Strunk, W., & White, E. B. *The elements of style.* New York: Macmillan Publishing Co., 1972.

Chapter 4
Using Graphs and Tables To Present Data

"It is sometimes said that the facts speak for themselves. In reality, statistics often stand speechless and silent, tables are sometimes tongue-tied, and only the graph cries aloud its message."[10]

This chapter offers guidance in the presentation of tables and figures. Properly constructed and described, tables and figures not only convey the major data summaries of your written evaluation report, they also provide the *visuals* for an oral one. For this reason, the best approach to preparing the *Results* and *Discussion* portions of your evaluation report—and sometimes other sections as well—is to *construct tables and graphs first*.

Begin by compiling all your summarized data—descriptions of the program, data summary sheets for questionnaires, computer printouts of achievement test results, etc. Then for each evaluation question you have chosen to answer,[11] find the set of graphs and/or tables that you think will most effectively portray what you have found. Some evaluation designs and certain types of measurement instruments lend themselves almost exclusively to one type of graphic or tabular presentation. In the case of, say, objectives-based tests or true control group evaluation designs, then, some of the graphs in your report will have been determined for you.[12]

---

10. Glass, G. V., & Stanley, J. C. *Statistical methods in education and psychology.* Englewood Cliffs, NJ: Prentice-Hall, 1970, p. 42.

11. The Results and Discussion questions in Chapter 2 are reminders of the sorts of questions your data might have to address.

12. Results from objectives-based tests are usually displayed via a *bar graph* like those on pages 60 to 63. Results from a true control group evaluation design, though they can be analyzed and presented in various supplementary ways, are first presented using the format of Table 7, page 55. Information about graphs and tables for presenting data from various designs and types of tests and attitude instruments can be found in Fitz-Gibbon, C. T., & Morris, L. L. How to design a program evaluation, and Henerson, M., Morris, L. L., & Fitz-Gibbon, C. T. How to measure attitudes. In L. L. Morris (Ed.), *Program evaluation kit.* Beverly Hills: Sage Publications, 1978.

Once you have roughed out your graphs and tables, you can organize your report around them, arranging them into a logical order and writing supporting text to explain each one.

When in doubt about whether you should use tables or graphs to summarize results, you are strongly advised to choose *graphs*. As the quotation chosen for the beginning of this chapter says, graphs make data clear and draw attention to important results—at least when they are correctly constructed. People leafing through an evaluation report generally pause longest to examine graphs. Not only can graphs clearly convey information to audiences, they also help the evaluator to explore and analyze the data and look for trends to help interpret what happened.

So that you can choose graphs and tables that will clarify data for both yourself and your audiences, the following pages describe various kinds of tabular and graphic data displays. Before you begin graphing, charting, and displaying, however, remind yourself of an important axiom:

You can expect that some of your readers will look only at the graphs and tables in your report without reading the surrounding text. Because of this, every graph and table should be self-explanatory. This requires a complete title, full labeling, a key to explain symbols, and footnotes with commentary about, for instance, missing data or statistical significance. On the other hand, not everyone can read tables and graphs; some people will rely on the text. The text too, therefore, should describe and discuss at least the key results presented in the visuals, mentioning the important numbers—means, correlation coefficients, and the like.

Tables

Everyone knows what a table is, and you need little instruction about how to construct one. But to save you the trouble of having to invent usable formats, and to introduce a few customary practices accompanying the use of tables, this section describes some which commonly appear in evaluation reports.

Some tables dealing with program implementation

If it is possible to describe the various components of a program succinctly enough to list them, then tables based on the list can be used to describe the program, show the results of its formative monitoring, and report summative evaluations of the adequacy of its implementation.

Table 1 shows a simple format for describing the principal features of a school program. When a program has *a few* distinguishing features, such a table could appear in the Program Description (Section IID, Chapter 2)

TABLE 1
Program Ex-Cell Implementation Description

Program Component:
4th Grade Reading Comprehension--Remedial Activities

Person responsible for implementation	Target group	Activity	Materials	Organization for activity	Frequency/duration	Amount of progress expected
Teacher	Students	Vocabulary drill and games	SMA word cards, 3rd & 4th level vocabulary	Small groups (based on CTBA vocabulary score)	Daily, 15-20 minutes	Completion of SMA, Level 4, by all students
			Teacher-developed word cards, vocabulary	Same	Same	None specified
			Old Maid	Same		None specified
Teacher/Aide	Students	Language experience activities--keeping a diary, writing stories	Student notebooks, primary and elite typewriters	Individual	Productions checked weekly (Fridays); students work at self-selected times or at home	Completion of at least one 20-page notebook by each child; 80% of students judged by teacher or aide as "making progress"
Reading specialist/teacher, student tutors	Students	Peer tutoring within class, in readers and workbooks	United States Book Company Urban Children reading series and workbooks	Student tutoring dyads	Monday through Thursday, 20-30 minutes	Completion of 1+ grade levels by 80% of students
Principal	Parents	Outreach--inform parents of progress; encourage at-home work in Urban Children texts; hold two Parents' nights; periodic conferences		All parents for program come to Parents' Night; other contact with parents on individual basis	Two Parents' Nights--Nov. and Mar.; 3 written progress reports in Dec., Apr., June; other contact with parents ad-hoc	

segment of the report.[13] Programs with long lists of activities and materials will make it necessary to place the table in an appendix.

An interim formative report, about how faithfully the program's *actual* implementation conforms to such a plan, or the progress the staff is making in carrying out activities on schedule, might look like Table 2.

TABLE 2
Project Monitoring--Activities[14]

Objective 6: By February 29, 19YY, each participating school will implement, evaluate results, and make revisions in a program for the establishment of a positive climate for learning.

Winona School District
Wiley School

Activities for this objective	Sep	Oct	Nov	Dec	Jan	Feb	Mar	Apr	May	Jun
		19XX				19YY				
6.1 Identify staff to participate		I	C							
6.2 Selected staff members review ideas, goals, and objectives		I	P	P	C					
6.3 Identify student needs		U	I	P	C					
6.4 Identify parent needs		U	I	P	C					
6.5 Identify staff needs		U	I	P	C					
6.6 Evaluate data collected in 6.3 - 6.5						I	U	C		
6.7 Identify and prioritize specific outcome goals and objectives			I	U	P	P	C			
6.8 Identify existing policies, procedures, and laws dealing with positive school climate		U	I	P	P	C				

Evaluator's Periodic Progress Rating:
  I = Activity Initiated   P = Satisfactory Progress
  C = Activity Completed   U = Unsatisfactory Progress

A formative evaluator can use this table to report the results of monthly site visits to both the program director—the district's Assistant Superintendent for Instruction—and the staff at each location. Each brief interim report consists of a table, plus footnotes explaining why ratings of "U," unsatisfactory implementation, have been assigned.

Table 2 can be modified for summative reports by assigning an overall letter or number "grade" to the program, or to each site, showing how adequately or accurately each program component has been implemented.

---

13. If a program's features either were not specified in advance, or if the program deviated widely from what was planned, it may become the job of the *evaluator* to describe the program's ultimate form. In this case, of course, Table 1 might appear in the Results section of the report.

14. This table has been adapted from a formative monitoring procedure developed by Marvin C. Alkin.

TABLE 3

Evaluation Assessment Plan

Program Objective	Type of Data	Assessment Tools	Population Assessed	Assessment Dates			Reporting Method & Date
				Pre	Interim	Post	
Second and third grade students participating in the bilingual-bicultural program will have a mean score of 20 or higher on the Rose-Smith Test of Awareness of Cultural Similarities and Differences	Formative	Rose-Smith Test of Awareness of Cultural Similarities and Differences	Sample (n=2 class-rooms at each site randomly chosen for each adminis-tration) of second and third grades in program only	9/28	11/20 1/15 3/18	5/31	Interim re-ports 12/1 and 4/19 Final report 6/21
The median percentile rank in reading com-prehension for third grade students will be 8 points higher on the posttest given in May than the pretest given in October to the same students	Summative	Comprehensive Test of Basic Abilities, Form K	All program third graders; sample of 45 non-program third graders in the district whose background is bilingual	9/12		5/10	Final report 6/21

This table would simply list each component and its assigned grade. Accompanying narrative would explain how the grade or implementation index was determined.

Tables describing the evaluation

A table is a concise way of giving the audience an overview of the activities *you* have or will undertake as evaluator—the tests given, observations made, reports delivered. A display like Table 3 summarizes your data collection and reporting plans per objective.

Allotment of time to various evaluation tasks is displayed by a Task-Timeline such as Table 6, page 54. A timeline might also be useful for showing *program implementation,* particularly if the program is to be in segments or phases or if certain activities are to be confined to specific time periods.

Tables showing attrition

Tables such as 4 and 5 usually are the first to appear in the *Results* section.

TABLE 4
Number of Students Dropped
From the Analysis for Various Reasons

Reason	Number droppped from Experimental Group (n=75)	Number dropped from Control Group (n=80)
Absent for posttest	6	5
Absent from school during the program	3	3
Removed from group at request of parent	1	0
Left school	4	1
Other reasons	0	2
Total number dropped	14	11

TABLE 5
Teachers Remaining After Three Stages
of Teacher In-Service Program

	Number of teachers who registered to attend workshops	Number and % who completed all workshops	Number and % who completed course requirements and received credit
Volunteers	80	73 (91%)	50 (63%)
Attendance required	96	69 (72%)	69 (72%)

TABLE 6
Evaluation Timeline

Tasks/Activities	Time in Months 19XX J J A S O N D J	Time in Months 19YY F M A M	Completion Date	Reports and Deliverables	Program Evaluator	Program Director	Teaching Staff	Principals	Teacher Aides	Clerical Staff
Review/revision of program plan	I		July 31	Revised written plan	37	8	-	6	-	16
Discussion about method of formative feedback alternatives	H		Sept 15	None	16	7	24	6	-	-
Planning of implementation-monitoring activities	I		Sept 30	List of instruments; Schedules of classroom visits	60	10	24	-	-	2
Construction of implementation instruments	I		Oct 10	Completed instruments	60	5	12	-	-	16
Planning of unit tests	I		Oct 10	List and schedule of achievement tests	30	5	-	-	-	2
First meeting with staff		—	Nov 1	None	9	15	24	2	20	-
First meeting with district administration		—	Nov 8	First interim report	22	20	-	-	-	30
TOTAL PERSON HOURS										

Number of personnel work hours consumed

Table for displaying pre- and posttest results

TABLE 7
Pre- and Posttest Results
for Experimental (E) and Control (C) Groups

				Pretest				Posttest
	N	Mean	SD	t-test of difference between E- and C-group means	Mean	SD	t-test of difference between E- and C-group means
E-group	32	10	10	.90	90	9	5.1*
C-group	35	58	8		80	7	

*statistically significant at .05 level

Table 7 shows that tests have been administered to two groups—an experimental (E) group and a control (C) group. Table 7, and those that follow, appear in the *Results* section of the report. SD means standard deviation. The column at the far right under both Pretest and Posttest shows the value computed by a statistical test to determine the significance of the difference—a t-test in this case. The asterisk identifies significant results and footnotes their level of significance.

Table for displaying data from a series of measures over time, based on a time-series evaluation design

TABLE 8
Mean Scores of E-Group
on Vocabulary Quiz

	Before Program			After Program		
	Jan	Feb	Mar	Apr	May	Jne
E-group mean	20	25	30	50	55	60

Notice that the caption describing a table always appears *above* it, with the word TABLE completely capitalized. The first letter of each important word in the caption is capitalized as well.

Table for displaying test scores from a single group, before and after evaluation design

TABLE 9
Mean Pretest and Posttest Reading and Math Scores
for Schools in the XYZ Program

Group	n[a]	Pretest	Posttest	t-test for difference between pre- and posttest
			Reading	
School A	401	59.4	64.3	3.8*
School B	720	50.2	70.5	12.2*
School C	364	40.9	60.2	4.5*
			Math	
School A	461	63.2	70.1	2.4*
School B	726	58.4	71.2	3.1*
School C	362	32.9	33.4	0.8

[a]Number present for both the pre- and posttests, and therefore the students on whose scores the t-test was calculated

*significant at .05 level

This table, by the way, has a footnote which uses the letter a. It is standard practice to show footnotes alphabetically in tables, saving asterisks for indicating statistical significance.

Tables for presenting correlations

Correlation refers to the strength of the relationship between two measures. A high *positive* correlation means that people scoring high on one measure also score high on the other. A high *negative* correlation also shows a strong relationship but in the opposite direction. A zero correlation means that knowing a person's score on one measure does not educate your guess about his score on the other. Correlation is usually expressed by a *correlation coefficient,* a decimal between −1 and +1, calculated from the scores that a single group of people have produced on the two measures.

The *graph* for displaying a correlation is a familiar one. Its axes represent scores on the two instruments of interest. As in Figure 6, a straight line represents the approximate relationship apparent between the two sets of scores.

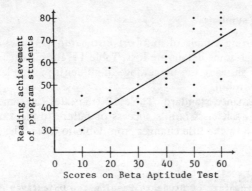

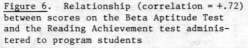

Figure 6. Relationship (correlation = +.72) between scores on the Beta Aptitude Test and the Reading Achievement test administered to program students

At times you may need to report several correlation coefficients—the relationships, perhaps, among all the instruments you have administered during the evaluation. You might want to do this, for instance, to show that your findings from various measures present a consistent picture, strengthening your conclusions. You might, as well, want to present a case for the validity of one of your instruments by showing that its results are related or unrelated to some of the *other* measures given to the same people. It could be, finally, that you want to show that people who score a certain way on one measure score predictably on one or more others. In any of these situations, you will want to construct a *table of correlations.*

Table 10, for example, contains a precise summary of a great deal of data on five measures. Besides students' mean scores on the various instruments, the table includes a correlation coefficient showing each measure's relationship to every other measure. The correlation between scores on the posttest and pretest is .76; between scores on the ability test and pretest, .38; between scores on the ability test and posttest, .49, etc.

TABLE 10
Means, Standard Deviations and Correlations Among Measures Used for the Evaluation

Measure	n	Mean	SD	Correlations 1	2	3	4
1 Pretest	55	13.5	6.1				
2 Posttest	55	23.1	12.9	.76*			
3 Ability test	55	18.9	6.5	.38*	.49*		
4 Effort rating	55	3.7	1.1	.42*	.50*	-.11	
5 Work done	55	25.1	17.8	.53*	.37*	.10	.27*

*p < .05

Tables containing symbols

Sometimes converting a table of numbers into *symbols* makes its message clearer even though some details are lost. Table 11, for instance, presents a format useful for showing the percentage of students passing key program objectives per classroom.

Using a performance standard, Table 12 translates the same data into symbols showing each classroom's success or failure to meet overall program goals. Note how the title changes from table to table. The first words

TABLE 11
Percentage of Students Passing the Objectives
in each of the Classrooms

Classroom	Writes name	Knows colors	Reads lower-case letters	Reads capitals
1	99	85	83	70
2	98	87	82	60
3	98	80	78	65
4	90	78	60	69
5	95	82	72	79
6	99	90	87	80
7	92	85	60	65
8	98	82	90	76
9	99	87	84	70
10	99	87	81	62

TABLE 12
Objectives Passed by 80% or more
of the Students in the 10 Classrooms

Classroom	Writes name	Knows colors	Reads lower-case letters	Reads capitals
1	+	+	+	o
2	+	+	+	o
3	+	+	o	o
4	+	o	o	o
5	+	+	o	o
6	+	+	+	+
7	+	+	o	o
8	+	+	+	o
9	+	+	+	o
10	+	+	+	o

KEY: + = objective passed by 80% or more of the students
      o = objective passed by less than 80% of the students

of the title usually refer to the numbers found in its body, but addition of symbols makes this difficult. Table 11 shows actual quantities of students passing classroom objectives. Table 12 uses a criterion set at 80% of students passing to show which classes meet program goals.

In the next section, which deals primarily with graphs, you will find a few additional examples of tables from which exemplary graphs have been constructed.

Graphs

Bar graphs

Bar graphs are common in evaluation and research reports—and for good reason. They are easy to understand. The data in Table 13 have been graphed to produce Figure 7.

TABLE 13
Mean Posttest Scores of Children
Who had or had not Participated
in the Cross-Age Tutoring Project

Group	n	Mean score[a]
Older children		
participants (tutors)	8	30.3
non-participants	14	15.8
Younger children		
participants (tutees)	24	18.1
non-participants	25	18.3

[a]The highest mean score possible was 36

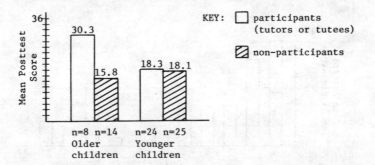

Figure 7. Mean posttest scores of children who had or had not participated in the cross-age tutoring project

While examining the table and graph in the above example, take note of the following:

1. A graph is called a *figure* when labeled and referred to in text. The caption for a figure is placed *under* it, and only the word Figure and the first word of the caption are capitalized.

2. In both tables and graphs, the main comparisons of interest are kept adjacent. The principal aim in Table 13 and Figure 7, for instance, is to compare posttest scores of tutoring program participants with those of non-participants—not to compare older students with younger ones. Therefore, *age* is used as the *first* division, naming the major titles of the table and defining the horizontal axis of the graph. *The evaluator, then, can place indicators of participation*—numbers in the table and bars in the graph—*close together.*

3. A key is provided for the bar graph.

4. To provide precise information, means per group are shown above the bars in the graph.

5. Both the table and the figure indicate the number of cases, n, on which each mean is based.

TABLE 14
Mean Percent of Students in Program X
Achieving the Twelve Objectives at Pretest

Group	Objective #											
	1	2	3	4	5	6	7	8	9	10	11	12
Ninth grades (n=23)	91	76	34	33	38	16	13	7	56	16	22	0

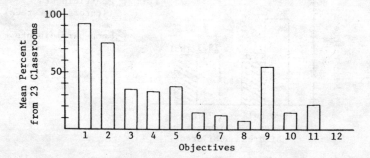

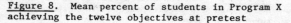

Figure 8. Mean percent of students in Program X achieving the twelve objectives at pretest

Bar graphs are particularly useful for presenting data about the achievement of objectives. If the graph has been constructed so that each bar represents one objective, a quick glance can pick out the strengths and weaknesses of a program.

Table 14 presents the data from which Figure 8 was drawn. Notice how much easier it is to see the pattern of achievement from the figure.

If both a pretest and a posttest have been given, the scores from both can be shown on the graph. In Figure 9, posttest results for each objective in Figure 8 have been added as shaded bars. The difference between the heights of the plain and shaded bars shows for which objectives there has been an increase in the number of students passing. Gains have been made mainly in objectives 5, 6, and 7.

TABLE 15
Mean Percent of Students in Program X
Achieving the Twelve Objectives at Pretest and Posttest

Group												

					Objective #							
Group	1	2	3	4	5	6	7	8	9	10	11	12
Ninth grades (n=23)												
pretest	91	76	34	33	38	16	13	7	56	16	22	0
posttest	77	62	43	41	66	35	30	11	30	7	7	2

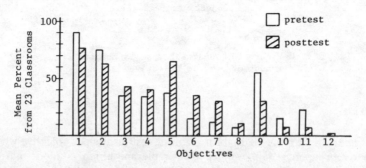

Figure 9. Mean percent of students in Program X achieving the twelve objectives at pretest and posttest

The type of graph shown in Figure 9 can also be used to display test
scores from *two groups*—an experimental and a control group, for example:

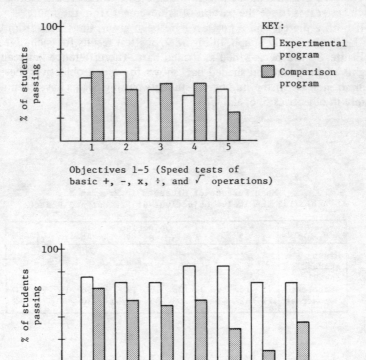

Figure 10. Posttest results for two
groups of program objectives

Figure 11 shows a method for graphing test results per objective when a
general program *goal* prescribes a desirable amount of student mastery.
For some objectives, the goal of a 100% pass rate may have been set. It
might have been decided, for example, that *all* students should be able to

read traffic signs accurately or know how to make change. For other program objectives, a goal of 80% of students passing might have been set; and for some objectives, mastery might be expected from only 20% of the students. This low expectation might correspond to the enrichment part of a curriculum. Pass rate expectations provide a way of *grouping* objectives as is illustrated in the example. Figure 11 also shows a particularly clear way of displaying pre- and posttest pass rates; posttest results are graphed as a shadow bar *behind* the pretest bar for each objective.

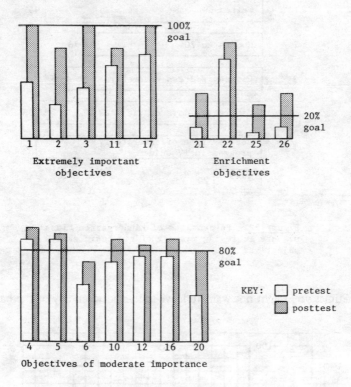

Figure 11. Achievement of program objectives showing different goals for the percent of students achieving the objectives

You can readily see from the figure that:
- The goal of 100% passing was not reached for objectives 2 and 11.
- The goal of 80% passing was not achieved for objective 6.
- Three goals had been achieved at pretest time—those for objectives 4, 5, and 22.

Putting a bar graph sideways is often convenient because it allows you to type labels inside the bars.

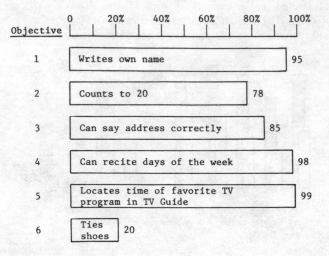

Figure 12. Percentages of kindergarten class members achieving mastery of six basic skills objectives

Sometimes you might not want to leave spaces between any of the bars:

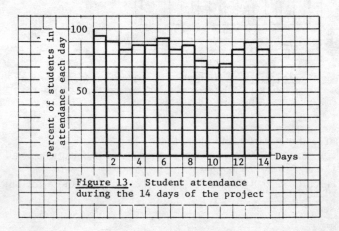

Figure 13. Student attendance during the 14 days of the project

Sometimes you might leave out the vertical lines dividing the bars altogether:

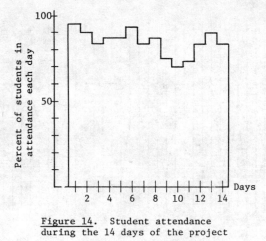

Figure 14. Student attendance
during the 14 days of the project

If the horizontal axis represents a measure that has a natural sequence, such as time or scores, you may wish to use a *line graph* rather than bother with bar graphs:

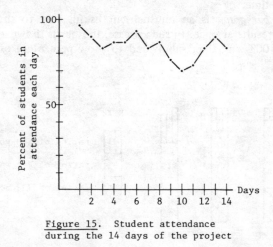

Figure 15. Student attendance
during the 14 days of the project

The line graph is particularly useful for showing results from *two or more* groups across time. Suppose, for example, you have attendance data from the experimental group, and you also want to show the attendance data of the comparison group students. The two attendance lines can easily be displayed together in the same graph as in Figure 16. Superimposing two bar graphs would be confusing.

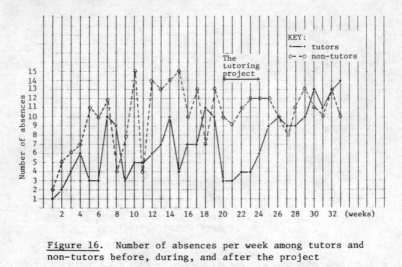

Figure 16. Number of absences per week among tutors and non-tutors before, during, and after the project

Since the horizontal axis is divided according to weeks, you have a display of trends over time.

A *divided bar graph* is an unusual but useful way to show several categories of results at once. In such a case, the bar is drawn to a length representing 100% and then subdivided to show percentage of results in each category.

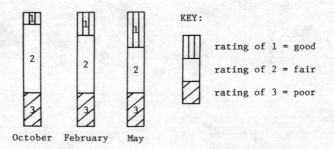

Figure 17. Percentage of students rating cafeteria food good, fair, or poor on three occasions

If the evaluator had graphed only the percent of students rating the food as *poor*, little evidence of change would have been apparent. By using the divided graph to display all three responses, however, he has been able to show that the proportion of *good* ratings steadily increased. It looks as if some of the students originally responding *fair* were won over, and began to respond good, while the solid group of poor responders did not change its mind.

A divided bar graph is a good way to display grade distributions.

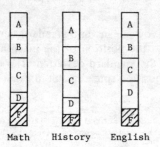

Math   History   English

Figure 18. Distribution of teacher–assigned grades in math, history, and English for the 10th grade

Because a grade of *F* is an *alarm signal,* it has been emphasized in the graph.

Showing the spread of scores

A deficiency of many graphs that show mean or average scores is that they fail to show the *dispersion* of scores—how much the scores tend to vary from the group average. This is unfortunate because indicators of score spread are easy to display.

A display of dispersion tells the audience how well the average represents the whole collection of scores. If dispersion is wide and scores vary considerably, then a mean or median must be considered less representative than when scores cluster near to it. The statistic which measures whether or not scores spread out widely around the *mean* is the standard deviation. On a *bar graph,* the standard deviation can be shown by a dotted line extending above and below the mean.

If the mean number of absences in a group was 20 with a standard deviation of 5, this could be shown in the following way:

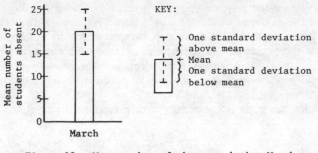

Figure 19. Mean number of absences during March

Another way to show means and standard deviations is by a *position spread graph*. It shows the position of the mean and the spread of scores around the mean via the standard deviation. The data shown in Table 16 are displayed on the position spread graph in Figure 20.

TABLE 16
Mean Scores on Attitude to
Tutoring Instrument of Students Receiving
20-, 30-, and 40-Minute Lessons

| | Length of Lesson | | |
	20 mins.	30 mins.	40 mins.
Mean	14.9[a]	16.1	13.7
Standard deviation	3.5	2.8	3.4
Number of students	30	18	10

[a]Maximum score=20

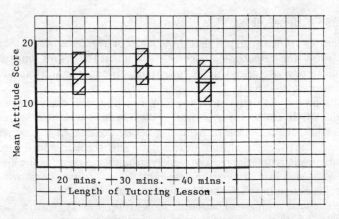

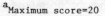

Figure 20. Mean scores on Attitude to Tutoring Instrument
of students receiving 20-, 30-, and 40-minute lessons

Displaying Results From Questionnaires

Questionnaire results can be tabulated—and therefore displayed and reported—in one of two ways:

1. *Responses to each question are examined separately.* The answers that each group of respondents made to each question are considered important enough to be displayed and discussed individually. This is the case with questions that ask about opinions or practices that are themselves either implementation or outcome objectives of the program. For example:

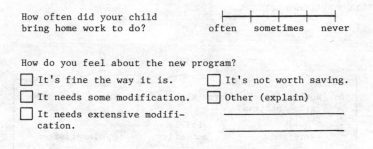

2. *Responses to two or more questions are added together or combined in some other way to produce an index of the degree to which people hold an attitude or possess a trait.* This is the case with *attitude rating scales,* special questionnaires constructed by means of an item selection method that allows results from several items to be combined to yield an indicator of say, "attitude toward school," "self-concept," or "vocational interest." The result produced by an index or attitude rating scale is a single number. Data from these instruments can be displayed using the tables and graphs described in the previous section.

When responses to *single questions* are to be discussed, it is customary to report *average responses* to the question per group, or *number* or *percentage* of respondents in each group answering a certain way. Averages are appropriate only for certain sorts of questions; percentages are almost universally applicable. You can report averages only where it makes sense to average—in cases where possible responses to the question reflect a *progression* in degree of attitude or behavior. For example:

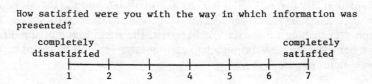

Reporting that parents in the program group gave a mean response of 6.2 to this question (standard deviation, 0.16) allows your audience to conclude that parents' general attitude was favorable. Average response could not be computed for a multiple choice question or one that asked for an answer of yes or no.

Most questions can be summarized by reporting the number or percent per group responding a certain way. Percentages are preferred because they make it easy to compare numbers from different sized groups.

The simplest way to present questionnaire data is to put summary statistics—the average response, or the number and percentage of persons choosing a particular response—directly onto a reproduction of the questionnaire as shown here:

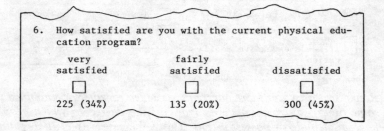

Notice that in this example reporting an *average* response would have obscured the fact that respondents fell roughly into two disagreeing groups. Some were satisfied and others dissatisfied.

Questionnaires made up of *several items reported individually,* but each represented by an average, lend themselves to *line graphs,* such as Figure 21. In constructing this graph, a mean response to each question has been computed for each group. These averages were then located on a copy of the questionnaire and included in the evaluation report. The graph seems to show little difference between the responses of the E- and C-groups except that the C-group tends not to like math lab and the E-group does. These conclusions have been drawn, of course, by simply looking at the graph—"eyeballing" the data. To be strict, the significance of the difference between the mean responses to each question should be tested before firm conclusions are drawn.

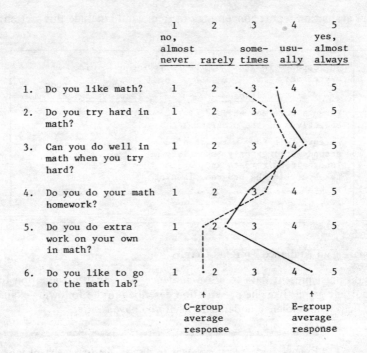

Figure 21. Mean responses of experimental (E) group and comparison (C) group to end-of-program math attitude questionnaire

If you want to display the *number or percent of the time* certain statements were made in response to *open-ended questions,* this can be done in table form. Instruments of this type are usually scored by underlining key statements in the answer given by each respondent. After a count has been made of recurrent statements, they are paraphrased as accurately as possible, and simply listed with their frequencies.

For instance, suppose you asked this question:

10. If there is something on your mind not covered by the questionnaire--either something you are especially pleased with or something you are concerned about--please let us know by writing in this space and on the back of the page.

Your evaluation report concerning this item would include this section:

```
In response to Item 10, the following criticisms were
expressed:
                                      Number of people
              Criticism              expressing criticism

Parents were not advised of the           5
objectives of the program

Parents felt they were asked to           4
attend meetings only to satisfy
funding requirements and not to
take part in the program planning
process

etc.
```

Preparing an Audience To Read Graphs

If you must present data to a live audience, a gradual introduction to an important graph, like the presentation described in the following example, will help your audience understand what you have to say:

Example. An evaluator wishes to display the line graph of tutor and non-tutor absence rates that was shown in Figure 16 of this chapter. He wants to be sure the graph is fully understood. He knows that at first glance, projected on a screen, the graph will look confusing. So he designs a presentation that will build up to the graph. First, he shows the axes of the graph and discusses them, pointing as he talks:

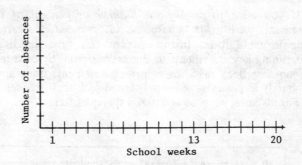

"This axis (the horizontal) represents school weeks; this is the first week of school (pointing to the "1" on the axis), and these are the 13th and the 20th weeks. For each week, the number of absences among the tutors was counted. The same was done for non-tutors.

"Absences are shown by the vertical axis. Suppose there was one group of students, say Group A, who were absent much more than another group, Group B. Then on the graph, their absence rates might look like this:

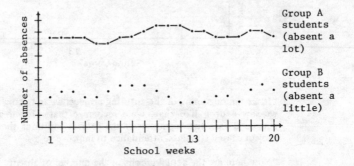

"Suppose that absenteeism increased steadily throughout the year. Then we'd see a rising line from week 1 to the end of the year, like this:

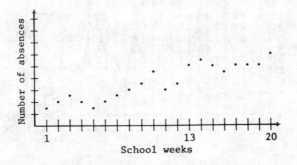

"The line is drawn zig-zag because there are always ups and downs, but the general trend is up, as you can see.

"Now suppose the school, at week 13, did something to lower the absence rate. Perhaps every school day was a party day. Then we'd expect the line to drop somewhere right at or after week 13.

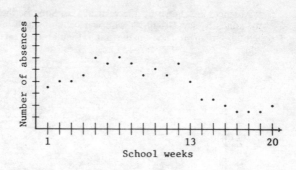

"If, at the beginning of the tutoring projects we're talking about today, we saw a drop like that, we'd recognize that a lower absentee rate coincided with the beginning of the project and think that perhaps the project caused students' attendance to improve.

"Now here are the actual graphs of the number of absences per week of tutors and non-tutors:

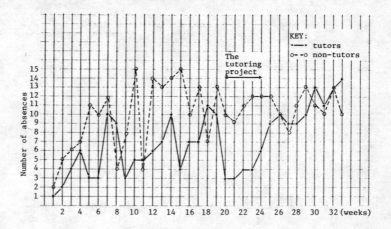

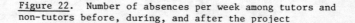
Figure 22. Number of absences per week among tutors and non-tutors before, during, and after the project

"Notice how the absence rate for *tutors* dropped noticeably during the project—right from its beginning. Then after the project, it climbed back up to being as high as the non-tutors.' Notice, too, the general increase in absence throughout the 33 weeks."

Here is another example, a brief one, in which the evaluator takes time to introduce the units used for the graph—percentile ranks in this case. His particular approach to interpreting percentiles may not be familiar to his audience.

Example. An evaluator wishes to show a parent advisory group the progress made by the district in improving students' percentile scores on a state-mandated achievement test. He has chosen the following novel way to represent percentile data:

"On a test whose scores have been converted to percentiles, a person can score anywhere from 0 to 100. Tests scored this way are set up so that a huge national testing would put 10% of all students into each of the 10 score categories shown here, 0 to 9, 10 to 19, etc. A graph of a nationwide testing, or from a school district with an average or normal range of students, would look like this:

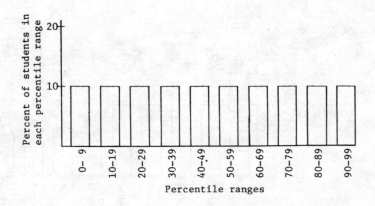

"That is, 10% of the students would be found in the top percentile range, 90-99 percentile, and 10% in each of the other divisions.

"However, ours being a below-average school district, the distribution we produced *last* year was as shown here:

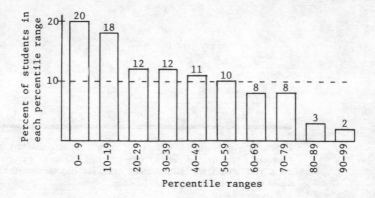

"We have *more students* in the lower achievement categories, the lower percentiles, than an average district would have, and we have correspondingly fewer students in the high categories. The aim of our program, then, has been to try to make our distribution look more like the first diagram and less like the second.

"*Here* are the results for this year. You can see we are getting closer to that 10% line right across the board":

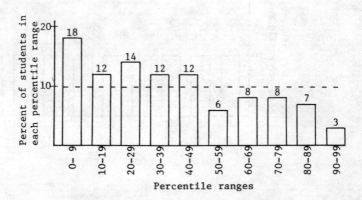

Presenting Data: A Summary

A glance through this chapter should give you some ideas about building tables and drawing graphs for your evaluation report. In particular, you are offered this advice:

1. Use graphic methods of presenting numerical data whenever possible.
2. Build the results and discussion section of the evaluation report—and perhaps other sections as well—around tables and figures. Prepare the tables and graphs first; then write text to explain them.
3. Make each table and figure self-explanatory. Use a clear, complete title, a key, labels, footnotes, etc.
4. Discuss in the text the major information to be found in each table and figure.
5. Play with, and consider using, as many graphs as you have the time and ingenuity to prepare. Not only do they communicate clearly to your audiences; they also help *you* to see what is happening.
6. Since graphs tend to convey fewer details than numerical tables, you may sometimes wish to provide tables *and* graphs for the same data.
7. When presenting complicated graphs to a live audience, give some instruction about how to read the graph and a few sample interpretations of simpler versions. Then present the real data.
8. When a complete draft of the report has been completed, ask yourself the following questions:

   • Is the title a comprehensive description of the figure? Could someone leafing through the report understand the graph?
   • Are both axes of every graph clearly labeled with a name?
   • Is the interval size marked on all axes of graphs?
   • Is the number of cases on which each summary statistic has been based indicated in each table or on each graph?
   • Are the tables and figures labeled and numbered throughout the report?
   • If the report is a large one, have you provided a *List of Tables and Figures* at the front of the report following the Table of Contents?

For Further Reading

Most introductory statistics books contain suggestions for constructing graphs and tables, as do the various style manuals listed at the end of Chapter 1. Look, in particular, at:

Glass, G. V., & Stanley, J. C. *Statistical methods in education and psychology.* Englewood Cliffs, NJ: Prentice-Hall, 1970.

Ingram, J. A. *Elementary statistics.* Menlo Park, CA: Cummings Publishing Co., 1977.

Index